Special Times for Infants

Ready-to-use assemblies for 4-7 year olds based on eight original songs, with additional resource material

Pamela Dew

Kevin Mayhew

First published in 2001 by
KEVIN MAYHEW LTD
Buxhall, Stowmarket, Suffolk IP14 3BW
E-mail: info@kevinmayhewltd.com

© 2002 Pamela Dew

9 8 7 6 5 4 3 2 1 0

ISBN 1 84003 849 7
Catalogue No 1500475

Cover design by Angela Selfe
Edited and typeset by Elisabeth Bates
Printed in Great Britain

Contents

Acknowledgements

I would like to thank the children of Broomgrove Infant School, Wivenhoe, for their enthusiastic and encouraging response to my songs over many years.

Also, thanks to Michael, my husband, for the research, editing and indexing that he carried out so generously.

Introduction

Involving younger children in a meaningful assembly is a demanding and most rewarding task, especially with the growing number of those who have very short attention-spans or exhibit unusual behavioural traits.

Leading an assembly or 'time of collective worship' specifically for 4-7 year olds calls for a much more instantly engaging approach than one for the full primary age range. For infants the moment is very transitory. This book will help you meet that challenge.

Following the publication of *Special Times* by Michael Dew (Eagle, 1997), which is on some county advisers' lists and still available, the need became apparent for more material to help with this younger age group. In discussion with teachers it appeared that music is of great interest to infant children and a useful vehicle to employ. So in this volume there are eight scripted assemblies, each based on an original song, specially written for and used successfully with Infants, Reception and Years 1 and 2. In addition, further assembly ideas for each of these eight themes are given, plus suggestions for other useful songs to employ in a similar fashion.

Narratives have a special appeal for young children, involving them personally and emotionally in an effective manner. Ways of using stories in assembly are discussed on page 53, with many titles listed from which you can choose.

Next, a whole range of suggestions is given of those tried and tested presentation strategies that are good infant practice in the classroom, and which can be successfully translated into assembly time.

The final section provides a list of other ideas that you can develop yourself into interesting assemblies.

Through these assemblies, underlying principles are laid whereby young children are encouraged to think for themselves and become aware that real science and following Jesus are quite compatible.

Infant assemblies can provide a variety of helpful opportunities that are shown in the diagram overleaf:

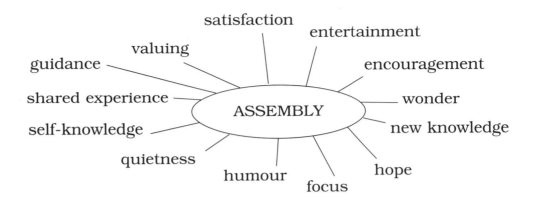

God's love and wisdom runs through all of these facets. Assembly can help children and adults to feel that they are valued members of the school family, as views and ideas which are important to them are expressed and explored.

Always seek to develop community spirit and relate assemblies to everyday life. Value imagination and contemplation, and show respect for everyone.

This is a challenging task, especially with reception children, and calls for thorough preparation, variety and adaptability. But your own sincerity and enthusiasm will be the foundation for a good presentation.

Each child needs to know that you are talking to him or her. Eye contact helps and occasionally asking a question of a child by name is useful. Questions asked of the whole school where only one or two may be chosen to answer usually means two happy children and 118 disappointed ones. Other ways of responding are outlined on page 65.

Watch the children's faces as you proceed and respond accordingly. Remember that *good things come in little parcels*, so keep to the point at all times and be succinct. Short talks linked with activities and involvement are to be preferred. If the children become restless, they may well be telling you something.

Aim to grab and keep their attention, making it more difficult not to listen than to listen!

Make the material that you use your own. To this end there is space provided in the script for your further notes and ideas (pages may be photocopied). Develop themes in a way that you think appropriate for your situation. The content should 'grow' or 'build up' to a climax. Any ideas, questions, tangential points and so on can be noted for a future assembly. Assemblies then become truly shared events and 'special times' together in school.

Using a song

Basing an assembly on a song is a good idea. It is effective because:

- children are involved with the words straightaway,
- the music adds drive and interest,
- the song, at least in part, is retained in the children's memory – the message of the song also stays with them,
- everyone is supporting everyone else – staff and children are listening and learning together,
- songs become favourites and can be enjoyed again.

The following eight assemblies provide ready-made material linked to a new song, plus further ideas for you to choose from and develop. The theme could be used for a week and the song repeated, thus adding it to your school's repertoire.

The songs are short and repetitive. They have all been used very successfully with 4-7 year old singers. It may be useful to work on learning a new song once or twice before using it in assembly.

When teaching a new song:

- First make sure that the children hear as full and accurate a performance of it as possible. Children have surprisingly good memories for tunes and ryhthms. For some, one hearing is enough and mistakes once learnt can be quite difficult to correct. If a pianist is not available, use the CD provided.

- Introduce one line at a time by singing it to the children and asking them to repeat it immediately.

- Start with the chorus if there is one. The youngest children can usually pick this up quickly and join in. Older pupils can carry the verse.

- Ensure every word and note is clear, taking a slower pace than normal.

- Write out a copy of the words that is large enough for all to see. It is worth the effort because this can be used in class music and literacy lessons.

Getting the children to listen well is the key to success. Infants often do this just as well and sometimes better than older children.

The children should be reasonably proficient before the song can be used in the assembly, but perfection is not essential.

Particular teaching points, where necessary, for each song are noted at the start of each assembly to aid successful preparation and practice with the children.

Singing a song again at the end of assembly is often appropriate too.

It is important that you make the assembly 'yours', so space has been given for other notes and ideas. Your own enthusiasm and honesty are paramount. Throughout the session(s) enjoyment and encouragement are both very important.

If you are an experienced teacher, the suggestions may seem over-prescriptive! For the benefit of newly qualified staff these assemblies are 're-lived' on the page, so that they can be presented by colleagues in varying situations with a similar vitality and success.

In the following eight assemblies each song is followed by a ready-made script (the bold words are suggestions as to what you might say), plus further ideas for development. The theme may then be used for a week or so.

Eight assemblies based
on original songs

Come back to school

Come back to school, the hol - i - days are o - ver, come back to school your friends are all here.

Come back to school, put on your shoes and coat and smile and learn some - thing new to - day.

Come back to school

Particular teaching points for song: none

Let's sing our song, it's a very jolly one – 'Come back to school'. After the song (repeating parts if you wish), continue:

Yes, holidays are over now, but this song reminds us of lots of things we love to do together here at school. Can we remember them together? What did we sing about?

Get as many of the list as you can, saying 'well done', etc., to encourage participation. The entire list is:

- painting
- bricks
- counting
- coloured sticks (or alternative)
- computer
- scissors and glue
- football or scoring goals
- pictures (with buttons, etc.)

Alternatively, to involve all the children, you can mime (or ask another teacher to) each of the activities and say, **Let's remind ourselves what we have sung about – there were lots of things. Say gently out loud all together the things I am (or Mrs X is) doing.** As you pretend to paint and the children say together words like 'painting' or 'making pictures' you respond mime by mime, keeping actions large and clear with **Yes, there was painting . . . and . . . building with bricks . . . and . . . counting . . . then . . .,** and so on, in a lively fashion, until they are all recognised, or nearly so. There is also mention of friends, smiling and learning something new in the verse. These may be missed, and you can ask a teacher to be ready to mention them if you like!

Thank you, everyone, for your help. Maybe your favourite thing at school was mentioned there. Let me read the list to you again.

Do so slowly and precisely. Ask the children to raise a hand when something they enjoy is read out, if they wish.

Maybe there are other things that you enjoy at school. Perhaps you will be able to talk about these in class. What a busy lot we are at school! I'm glad singing was a

favourite too. The song was a happy one, because we are all back together again, to work and play, and learn with our friends.

It's really wonderful that God has made us all able to do so many different things.

Either read 'Crayoning' by Stanley Cook (page 14, *A Very First Poetry Book*, OUP, 1984), or, 'School break' by Joan Poulson (page 22, *Another Second Poetry Book*, OUP, 1988). Both are compiled by John Forster.

Comment as appropriate, e.g. **This poem tells us how clever you are to make/crayon those lovely pictures you take home sometimes,** or **What a lot of games we can enjoy at playtime with our friends.**

To conclude, have a moment of silence, to think about all that is done in school, each child highlighting a favourite activity in their own mind.

We hope you all have a busy and interesting day, using all *your* skills and talents.

Further ideas

1. Ask a group of children in your class to tell or show what they are good at or enjoy, e.g. it may be using cuisenaire/ colour factor (as in the song), or investigating where snails live, or skipping, or writing stories . . .

2. Say a thank-you prayer for what each of them can do, and for the satisfaction they enjoy.

3. Suggest the children talk about this at home. They could tell their family what they think they are themselves good at, and then ask them to talk about their own abilities and interests.

4. 'Learning something new' – This happens so often at this age yet can go unrealised! Tell the children of an occasion when *you* learnt something new (preferably with a practical application). Try to get them to think hard about their own learning, as their knowledge and skills will grow day by day. What do they know today that they did not know last week? What can they do today that they could not do yesterday?

3. 'Our friends are here.' Discuss what the children have been doing as friends together in the playground and the classroom. Explain how activities like games and singing are so much more enjoyable in larger groups.

Shadows

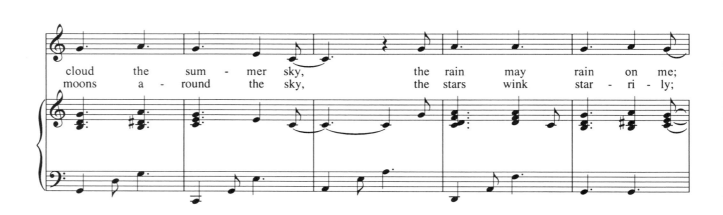

To repeat

sky my sha - dow keeps sha - dow-ing me. The

Last time | *To continue*

Sha - dows

big, sha - dows small, sha - dows all a - long the

gar - den wall; car - shaped, tree - shaped, you - shaped,

15

The clouds may cloud the summer sky,
the rain may rain on me;
but when the sun shines in the sky
my shadow keeps shadowing me.

The moon just moons around the sky,
the stars wink starrily;
but when the sun shines in the sky
my shadow keeps shadowing me.

Shadows big, shadows small,
shadows all along the garden wall;
car-shaped, tree-shaped, you-shaped, me-shaped;
shadows, shadows everywhere.

The clouds may cloud the summer sky,
the rain may rain on me;
but when the sun shines in the sky
my shadow keeps shadowing me.

Shadows

Particular teaching points for this song:

The last line ('My shadow keeps shadowing me') may require extra practice. Sing or play it to the children, paying attention to the rhythm and the semitones.

This is a longer assembly. Preferably use this song on a sunny day so the children can go out at some appropriate time and find shadows to play with.

On our summer holidays we went to a lovely little Greek island. It was sunny and I could look out of our front door and see the long shadows of the large pots on the terrace. Then one day I looked out and there were no shadows to see at all on the terrace! Why do you think this was?

Hopefully you will get answers like, 'The sun wasn't shining', or it had 'gone in', or 'it was cloudy'. Someone may even say, 'It was a different time of the day.'

Yes, that's right. It was a cloudy day and the sun was there but it couldn't be seen shining brightly – like it is today. . . . Let's sing about the shadows all around us.

Now sing 'Shadows'.

Now these shadows, why are they car-shaped, tree-shaped, you-shaped and me-shaped? Listen to, and repeat if you wish, the answers given, without any comment as to their scientific accuracy!

Then pose the question, **Can we make shadows in here, then?**

Shake your head if you think 'no', nod your head if you think 'yes'. Well some think 'yes' and some think 'no'. Let's try . . . I have a large lamp (a big hand-torch or a slide projector or an angled lamp), **a shadow screen, and some things and shapes here. Let's make some different shadow shapes. Who will help me?'** The hall will need to be blacked out, or if the sun is shining directly onto a wall you have a convenient alternative!

You can either take volunteers or preferably have some of your own class prepared and ready! The objects should be stored in a hidden place beforehand. Go through them one at a time, with your helpers holding the objects between the lamp and the screen, and then say, **Well, what is making this shape?** Children can respond gently out loud all together.

You respond: **Yes it's a book**, and your helper can show everyone what she/he is holding.

What about this shape – what can be making this shadow?, generating interest and involvement.

Proceed similarly through five or six of your selected objects and shapes. Don't deviate down side-tracks about the possible varying size of shadow according to where your helpers stand, or any slight distortions. Just note any comment and suggest that these points can be thought about later, or they can ponder the problems themselves.

You could also have a few children come out to create shadows of themselves . . . 'James'-shaped or 'Sonia'-shaped shadows.

Wow, all these shadows! At playtime, you try to get away from yours!

And here's something really worth thinking about. Parent birds spread out their wings in the nest and the little chicks huddle underneath for safety. David, the great king, once said, 'Hide me, Lord God, in the shadow of your wings' (Psalm 17:8). Think about that!

Further ideas

1. Poems to read, enjoy and talk about:

   'A clear day and a yellow sun' by Gregory Harrison (page 21, *A Very First Poetry Book*, OUP, 1984).

   'Copycat' by Robert Heidbreder (page 34, *The Oxford Treasury of Children's Poems*, OUP, 1988. Compiled by Michael Harrison & Christopher Stuart-Clarke).

   'My shadow' by Robert Louis Stevenson (page 35, *The Oxford Treasury of Children's Poems*; and page 28 in his own *Child's Garden of Verses*, Harrap, 1946; and also page 46 in *First Poems*, Orchard, 1993).

2. To help find an explanation for this assembly's final thought, ask the children what they do on a hot day to keep cool. The value of shade may then arise, and the shadows made by larger objects like trees and buildings may be looked at. The shadow of a rock on a very hot day is another picture of God's protection (Isaiah 32:2).

3. You may like to develop the theme by using poems to look at:

   Reflections: see 'My playmate' by Mary Osborn (page 34, *The Oxford Treasury of Children's Poems*) or

Echoes: 'Echoes and shadows' by Lydia Pender (page 36 in her *Morning Magpie* collection, Angus and Robertson, 1984).

4. The wonder and mystery of these elements of creation can help children begin to appreciate God's power and inventiveness. Talk together about what the children think God is like.

Keeping warm

Thoughtfully

1. How do worms keep warm?

How do worms keep warm? When the wind is blow-ing and the snow is snow-ing and the

long sharp ic - i - cles keep grow-ing and grow-ing, how do worms keep warm? They
(v.4 We)

Brighter

Verses 1, 2, & 3

all dig tun-nels in the cold dark ground and they stay deep down 'til spring comes a - round

Verse 4

That's how worms keep warm, yes, that's how worms keep warm. put on vests and pants and shirts and

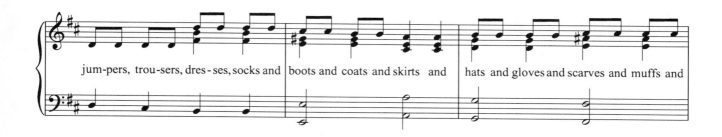

jum-pers, trou-sers, dres-ses, socks and | boots and coats and skirts and | hats and gloves and scarves and muffs and

CODA (optional)

clothes of ev - 'ry sort, yes, | that's how we keep | warm. We're

ve - ry co - sy, warm as toast and | snug as bugs in rugs, yes | that's how we keep | warm!

2. How do birds keep warm?
   How do birds keep warm?
   When the wind is blowing and the
   snow is snowing and the
   long sharp icicles keep growing and growing,
   how do birds keep warm?
   They preen their feathers and they
   smooth them all, and they
   puff them up like a fluffy, fluffy ball.
   That's how birds keep warm, yes,
   that's how birds keep warm.

3. How do cats keep warm?
   how do cats keep warm?
   When the wind is blowing and the
   snow is snowing and the
   long sharp icicles keep growing and growing,
   how do cats keep warm?
   They tiptoe lightly on the
   cold, white snow, and they
   'Miaow' at the window 'cos they want you to know,
   they'd like to come inside, yes,
   that's how cats keep warm.

4. How do we keep warm?........etc.

21

Keeping warm

An assembly for a cold day in winter.

Particular teaching points for this song: to enable young non-readers to join in from the start, focus first on the repeated phrases 'when the wind is blowing . . .'

QUESTIONS, questions, questions. March up and down in front of the children as you say this several times (seemingly to yourself), perhaps scratching your head or rubbing your chin.

Questions, questions, questions . . .
We all have them, don't we? (Turn to face the children now.) **'How' questions, 'why' questions, 'where' questions, 'what' questions, 'when' questions** (say slowly one by one) **. . . Questions? Yes, they help to find answers.**

Our question this morning is a 'how' question. What song have we recently learnt that is a 'how' question? Yes, 'How do worms keep warm?', then in the song, 'How do birds keep warm?', 'How do cats keep warm?'. Look and listen for the answers as we sing our song today.

Sing 'Keeping warm' leaving out verse 4 (which is almost a joke) till a later assembly, if you wish (see further suggestions).

Wow, isn't it amazing how each creature keeps itself warm in different ways? The worms know how to look after themselves, the birds know how to look after themselves and our cats know how to look after themselves. So do all sorts of other animals.

Let's remind ourselves together how they do it, the words are here still if you need them. (Point) **Say the answers to the 'how' questions with me, gently. How do worms keep warm? They dig tunnels in the cold dark ground. How do birds keep warm? They puff up their feathers in a fluffy ball, yes, and how do cats keep warm?** (with a giggle) **Yes, they ask to come inside.**

Say the answers clearly. The children's responses will vary a bit, but they are all able to be involved.

And what did the song say were the signs of a cold day? Say the words with me: 'When the wind is blowing and the snow is snowing.' Yes, that's right. (If you continue the refrain and mention the icicles, you may decide to explain what they are. Perhaps it is better to wait until there are some around for the children to see.)

So it was cold this morning. Think to yourself about what you did to keep warm; we shall talk about that tomorrow/next week/another day. For now, sit quietly, close your eyes if you like, and think about the animals that you know and how they keep warm. Thank God for them all . . .

Further ideas

1. 'How do we keep warm?' Before using the final verse in assembly to complete the song, children could talk about this with their own class teacher. Each class could bring an item of clothing to show. What a contrast to the animals! The verse is fun to sing, because there are so many words to fit in, and you can even try to match the items of clothing to the words.

2. Continuing questions and weather themes, read 'Wind ways' by Judith Nicholls (page 48, *Another First Poetry Book*, compiled by John Forster, OUP, 1992).

3. Make up another verse together in class/literacy time about another animal(s). Sing it to the whole school one day.

4. There are lots of links here with science topics – animals suited to habitats/warm- and cold-blooded animals/classification of mammals.

5. On the theme of wild and tame animals, *Paddiwak and Cosy* by Bertie Doherty (Little Mammoth, 1988) is a lovely story to read and talk about. It touches upon security and friendship.

6. On the theme of materials, the idea of clothes for different purposes can be the basis of another assembly. Children can parade dressed for a variety of occasions, e.g. for a winter walk, for the beach, for a party.

Bring in the harvest

Bring in the harvest

Particular teaching points for song – none.

Traditionally an assembly for the autumn term, but when stressing the abundance of food we consume from around the world it can be used at other times. Begin by slowly standing up and taking an apple out of a bag, carefully shining it, looking at it gleefully and preparing to bite it, mouth very wide! Hold position for a moment, change gaze from apple to the children.

Who likes apples? Put your hand up if you do – lots of you. Yes, it's a tasty fruit. Most children will probably put up a hand, but look for a few who haven't and ask them by name. **Which fruit do you particularly like then, Katie?** (and repeat reply). **Ah, bananas . . . and what's your favourite, Sanjay? Oranges, very nice,** and so on.

What a lot of different fruits there are too. Some we grow in this country, like apples and pears, others come from countries far away over the sea, like bananas/ peaches. (Perhaps have samples of each to hold up, as you talk, but keep the pace up.)

When the fruit is ripe it is picked; when crops in the field are ready they are gathered in. The potatoes are lifted by machines, and fish are caught at sea by fishermen in big boats. This we call the harvest. In our country this happens now, in August and September, but it happens all round the world at different times of the year.

Let's sing about all this; our song for today is 'Bring in the harvest, share out the harvest'. Sing whole song through twice.

If you want a slightly longer assembly, continue with option (i); if not, take option (ii).

(i) **What did we sing about that was cut? It was** (encourage children to say with you, by hand and face signals) **the wheat. Yes, WHEAT. I have some wheat here too** (hold up a few ears). **This grows in the fields, is cut and made into? If you know, say it together: it's made into . . . bread.**

Yes, bread is eaten all round the world. These stalks have little grains like this (show one) **in them, which are squashed down into flour** (show a packet, pour some out if you wish) **and then made into bread by the baker.**

The bread, some brown, some white, granary loaves, small rolls, olive bread, we can buy in the shops. You look out for the different ones and their names when you next visit the bakers or supermarket.

And . . . someone has worked hard to make all this bread (continue to ii).

(ii) **And someone has worked hard to grow and bring us all the food we sang about.**

Listen to this story that Jesus told long ago. Which brother really helped with the harvest?

Read Nick Butterworth's and Mike Inkpen's 'The two sons' (based on Matthew 21:28-32, Marshall Pickering, 1986).

People have to work hard so we can enjoy the food and we must all work hard to share what God has given us.

Now let's sit still and quiet and think about all the different foods we enjoy – fruit, bread, fish, sausages, vegetables . . . think of all the people who worked hard to grow the fruit and vegetables, to catch the fish and make the sausages and bread, we'll say a thank you prayer together. Join in and say 'Thank you, God' with me.

For all those who work hard to give us our food, THANK YOU, GOD. (Give a clear lead here.)

For all the different foods we have to enjoy and share, THANK YOU, GOD.

Further ideas

1. The variety of foods (not only breads) in the shops is fascinating for children to investigate. Teachers and assistants can start by bringing one item each from a different country and the whole school could collect for a while. We leave you to sort out the practicalities! But just looking at and talking about what they've found is great fun.

2. The taste of unusual fruits can be explored by the class, for example, kiwi fruit, pomegranite, guava, cherries can be compared with apple, orange, lemon, banana. At various times of the year, the list is endless. Cutting them up in front of the children and then, one by one, distributing and talking about the tastes and textures is great fun.

3. The whole idea of sharing the world's food is a subject some seven year olds can understand. With the pictures of hungry children often on television and the surplus of foods elsewhere, the question of how we can help and share is worth talking about. There is, after all, enough food in the world for everyone.

4. *Poems and Prayers for a Better World*, ed. Su Box and Felicity Henderson (Lion, 1999) is worth looking at, to find one or two items to read to the children.

Looking into space

Smoothly

1. I looked up at the sky a-bove and saw the moon,

shi - ning. Is it sil - ver or is it gold, is it hot or cold,

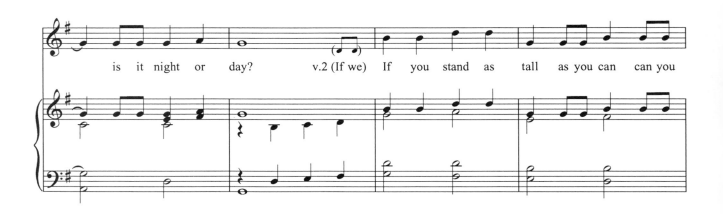

is it night or day? v.2 (If we) If you stand as tall as you can can you

reach the moon, near - ly? How can you fly up high in the sky and

land on the moon, far a - way?

A little quicker
Chorus

Climb a - board a

space-ship, hold on tight, we're rea-dy to go. 5 4 3 2 1 then lift - off,

earth is far be - low. Past the moon and on to Mars and the

29

Mil - ky Way with mil-lions of stars; space is bet-ter than choc -'late bars, an

as - tro - naut, that's me.

2. Out in space will there be a place
   where we could live, somewhere?
   If we raced through the cold black waste
   of outer space, would a home be there? If we
   took a flight at the speed of light through the galaxy, searching,
   is there a planet, globe or sphere
   like planet earth, our world so fair?

   Chorus.....

Looking into space

Particular teaching points for the song:
The chorus is easier than the verse and younger children will be able to listen out for and join in the 5, 4, 3, 2, 1. This is a wondering song, mixing fantasy and realism and posing questions that children readily ponder.

If possible, once the children are seated, darken the hall. Play some atmospheric space music that will immediately send the children's mind shooting off, for example, 'Space Odyssey 2001', or the opening track of *Hopes and Dreams* (musical by Paul Fields and Stephen Deal, Kingsway, 1999).

As the music fades or finishes, state the well-known words, **Space, the final frontier . . .** and slowly read out the names of the planets, **Saturn, Mars, Jupiter, Neptune, Venus, the sun and the moon.**

Allow a few quiet, wondering moments.

As we see the awesome size of space, out and up there (show with large sweeping arm movements) **we want to know more. I am going to read a story, which some of you may know: 'The bears who stayed indoors'** (Susannah Gretz, Puffin, 1972). Read the whole story and then remark, **There are lots of things we imagine about the planets and space; there are lots of questions still to be answered.**

Let's sing about this thoughtfully. Sing 'Looking into Space' (through twice if time) and end with **Maybe one day, *you* will find out some of the answers.**

We end our assembly with some wonderful words from the Bible:

God made the bright lights in the sky.
God's love never fails.
He lets the sun rule each day.
God's love never fails.
He lets the moon and the stars rule each night.
God's love never fails.

(Psalm 136:7-9, CEV)
(The children could be invited to join in the refrain.)

Further ideas

1. Other stories:

   Whatever Next (Baby bear travels to the moon and back) by Jill Murphy (Campbell Books, 1998).

   Dinosaurs and All That Rubbish by Michael Foreman (Picture Puffin, 1974).

2. 'Is space better than chocolate bars?' Galaxy, Mars, Milky Way . . . a little joke in the song using a pun, but older infants with discernment may like to talk about this, giving their opinions on both marketing techniques and space travel.

3. 'Twinkle, twinkle, little star' (page 162, *Oxford Treasury of Children's Poems*, 1988). This version is by Jane Taylor and is worth reading in full.

4. '5, 4, 3, 2, 1, lift-off.' For younger children, counting up and down the numbers (even from 20) is fun, with a jump up from the chair at the appropriate moment.

5. How many of the children visited the Millennium Dome? Maybe enough to talk together about the Space Journey experience, a quest to find a suitable home for humans.

   'Is there life elsewhere?' More able children can discuss what is fact and what is fiction. What is valid evidence anyway? They could search for help in books and newspapers. Visits to places like the Planetarium can also be discussed.

6. 'Is there another me?' Read and talk about John Rice's poem, 'On some other planet' (page 9, *First Poems*, Orchard, 1993).

Special Times
for Infants

The hungry caterpillar

Smoothly

The

sil - ver moon was shin - ing on an egg up - on a leaf: soon the
built a lit - tle house that had no win - dow and no door; a co -

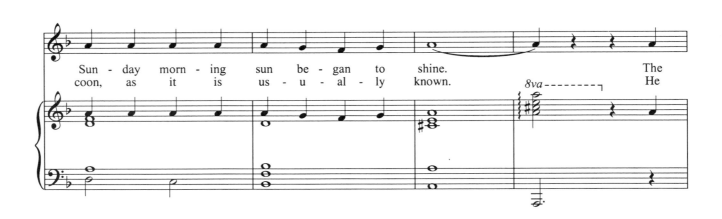

Sun - day morn - ing sun be - gan to shine.   The
coon, as it is us - u - al - ly known.   He

34

world was warm, the egg went 'pop!' a ti - ny head ap -
stayed in - side so qui - et - ly through - out two weeks or

peared, of a cat - er - pil - lar look - ing for some food.
more; made a hole and came out - side to show the world,

Jauntily
To verses

he'd be -

Fine

come a rain - bow col - oured but - ter - fly.

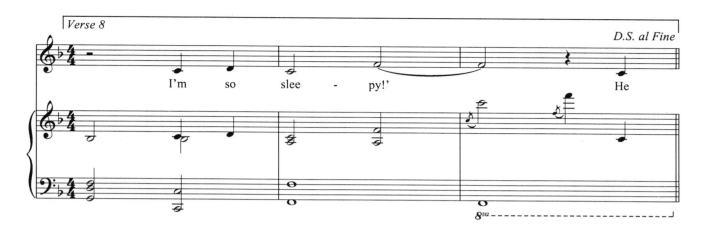

1. The silver moon was shining on an
   egg upon a leaf;
   soon the Sunday morning sun began to shine.
   The world was warm, the egg went 'pop!'
   a tiny head appeared, of a caterpillar
   looking for some food.

2. (*Monday) morning came around,
   he looked about and then he found
   (∆ one apple)
   He munched and crunched his tasty snack,
   went in at the front and out of the back of
   (∆ one apple)
   'cos he was hungry, very hungry.

3. *Tuesday...∆ two pears
4. *Wednesday...∆ three plums
5. *Thursday...∆ four strawberries
6. *Friday...∆ five oranges

7. On Saturday he ate all day
   through anything that came his way
   whatever.
   That night he had a stomach ache
   he knew that eating all that cake
   was greedy, very greedy, don't be greedy.

8. Sunday morning came again,
   he ate a leaf and then he felt much better.
   He wasn't hungry anymore,
   he'd never felt like this before;
   'I'm happy, I'm very happy.
   I'm so sleepy!'

9. He built a little house that had no window
   and no door;
   a cocoon, as it is usually known.
   He stayed inside so quietly
   throughout two weeks or more;
   made a hole and came outside to show the world,
   he'd become a rainbow-coloured butterfly.

The hungry caterpillar _____

Based on the book by Eric Carle (*The Very Hungry Caterpillar*, Puffin, 1970), this is a shorter assembly for summer.

Particular teaching points for this song – hold the book up and turn the pages as you sing it through for the first time.

Sing the song through first, turning the pages as you go.

This is really happening out there (point to window, school fields, for example).

Yes, out there, on plants and trees, caterpillars are munching away at the leaves. Different sorts of caterpillars like to eat different sorts of leaves. So, if you find a caterpillar and want to take it indoors for a while, look at what it is eating and take some of the same leaves with you for it to eat. Be careful and gentle with it too, won't you?

And how is it, I wonder, that although they only eat green leaves, the caterpillars end up as lovely brightly coloured butterflies? We don't know all about it, but perhaps you will find out one day. Look out for butterflies today or on sunny days and be still near them to get a good look at all the different patterns and colours in their wings.

Let's finish our assembly by being still and quiet and thinking about all the caterpillars and butterflies out there in the fields/the park/your gardens/the bushes by the school gate.

A time of quiet . . . Say 'Thank you, God' with me in this short prayer, if you wish:

For the wonders of your world,
THANK YOU, GOD.
For all the caterpillars that change
into colourful butterflies,
THANK YOU, GOD.

Further ideas

1. The children will begin to realise that creatures have preferred habitats and this can be further investigated together as a Science activity.

2. There are very good facilities available now for rearing and hatching your own caterpillars in school. This is a

wonderful experience for the children that ends with them sending the butterflies back to their own environment. If you do this, a report on progress can be made in this, or other assemblies.

One supplier is:
Insect Lore, PO Box 1420
Kiln Farm, MK19 6ZH
Tel: 01928 563338
www.insectlore.com
(about £40 for the full kit).

3. *The Very Hungry Caterpillar* story can be developed into a parents' assembly or concert item, illustrating the song with actions and props. Plastic PE hoops covered in tissue paper of different colours, representing each fruit, can be used very effectively for the caterpillar to go through.

And God said . . .

Steadily

1. And God said... 'Let there be light in my new world where

Last verse to Coda

night gives way to each new day.' And God looked at the light that he had made

CODA

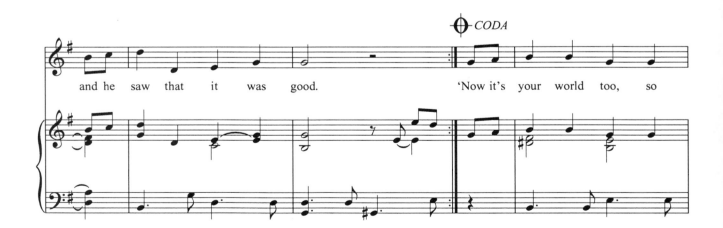

and he saw that it was good. 'Now it's your world too, so

please take care of all liv - ing kinds both great and small, I love them all.'

2. And God said...
   'Let there be space in my new world,
   a sky of blue, the deep sea too.'
   And God looked at the space that he had made
   and he saw that it was good.

3. And God said...
   'Let there be plants in my new world
   with flowers and leaves and fruits and seeds.'
   And God looked at the plants that he had made
   and he saw that they were good.

4. And God said...
   'Let there be stars in my new world,
   the sunshine bright, the moon by night.'
   And God looked at the stars that he had made
   and he saw that they were good.

5. And God said...
   'Let there be creatures in my new world
   to run, swim, fly and multiply.'
   And God looked at the creatures he had made
   and he saw that they were good.

6. And God said...
   'Let there be people in my new world,
   I'd like to share my world so fair.'
   And God said to the people living there,
   'Now it's your world too, so please take care
   of all living kinds both great and small,
   I love them all.'

And God said . . .

Particular teaching point for the song:
There is only one new line in each verse, so the first verse can be worked on more than the rest. However, the last verse is quite different.

Have an empty table beside you and an object that looks handmade like a vase or model (one of your own, if possible) hidden nearby. Children sitting in a semicircle as much as possible would be advantageous. This is a longer assembly.

Good morning, everyone. Please now close your eyes and keep very still.

Pause a few moments, then speak very slowly: **In the beginning, it was black, silence, there was nothing, nothing to make anything with, nothing at all. In the beginning God created the heavens and the earth out of nothing at all.** Try to ensure that the few open eyes don't see you place your hidden object on the table at this point.

Now, open your eyes. Look what I've made out of nothing. Point triumphantly to the object. There will be sighs of 'No you didn't, you can't have', etc.

No, of course, you are right (knowing smile). **But God did, really did; there's a song about it. Let's sing it now, just as the Bible tells us it happened.**

Sing the song all the way through.

Lovely, well done, everyone. What a wonderful world God made. But whose job is it to look after it now? Let the children speak all at once, then continue, **Yes, it's our job, it's mine** (point to yourself). **All of you, point to yourself and say with me, 'It's mine. Yes, it's mine.'**

Further ideas

1. Read 'I wonder' by Jeannie Kirby (page 57, *Oxford Treasury of Children's Poems*).

2. The responsibility of caring for the world is a complex issue. But practical ideas can be discussed and put into practice by children, parents and staff in your own school grounds. Maybe a long-term project will result that will be an environmental resource for years to come.

3. See *Poems and Prayers for a Better World,* ed. Su Box and Felicity Henderson (Lion, 1999), especially page 11, Steve Turner's 'I like the world'.

4. Read *Dinosaurs and All That Rubbish* by Michael Foreman (Picture Puffin, 1974).

5. Children can be encouraged, with their families, to look after the natural world in their own gardens and join in wider local community activities. Your local council's Environmental Officer will help with information.

Stop, look, listen

Steady walking pace

The sun is shin-ing bright-ly so the park is where we'd like to go; it's down the road, not far now; oh it's

on the oth-er side. So we STOP, LOOK, LI-STEN for bus-es, lor-ries, bikes and cars, we

STOP, LOOK, LI-STEN and walk a-cross the road. road.

Notes:-

1) More verses can be sung by exchanging 'park' for another place e.g. 'zoo', or 'shops'.

2) When the children can sing the melody with confidence, the piano accompanist need not follow the tune, but could play more of the piece in the 'stride' style of the first three bars, as appropriate.

Stop, look, listen

Particular teaching points for this song: the tune of the verse needs care, there are semitones and a change of key back and forth.

An assembly for Child Safety Week, perhaps.
Let's sing our song first today, it's 'Stop, look, listen'.
After the song, the main ingredient is a teacher-led drama. If space can be found in the hall, a road scene can be set up with things like traffic lights and kerbs marked out. Traffic can be provided by bikes and cars ridden by the early-years children.

Alternatively children can walk along and pretend to be vehicles, with appropriate sounds if you wish. Cast, in addition to the above, is a lollipop lady ready and waiting and a group of children.

The story will have to fit your specific local situation, so invent it in more detail for yourself. The main thread is that the children are playing with a balloon in a garden. The balloon floats out into the road and is run into by a vehicle and bursts. Very dramatic, as it pops!

The teacher narrates the story at a steady pace, and uses the punch line at the end.
That could be you . . . we are all much more precious than a balloon or ball. You can always get another balloon, but there's only one you. If you wish, now include a short prayer: **Lord, please keep us all safe on the roads and in our streets.**

Pause, look around, intently concerned, at all the faces. If you wish, now sing the song again to finish.

Further ideas

1. The lollipop lady in the drama was very prominent but not used. In class, explain her role in keeping children safe.

2. Obeying rules is important. Talk about why this is so. Breaking rules brings danger. Share examples. God gives us helpful rules for our lives. Read 'Michael bumps his head', page 14 in Brian Ogden's *It's a Big Family* (Lord's Prayer) (Bible Reading Fellowship, 1999).

3. Use local contacts to widen the matter to general safety for people, adults and children, e.g. fire safety, water safety, safety in the home, stranger danger, taking medicines, dogs. Many people will be only too delighted to visit your school.

4. Read 'The house on the rock' from *Stories Jesus Told*, by Nick Butterworth and Mike Inkpen (Marshall Pickering, 1994).

Other songs on which to base an assembly

Details of music source books are listed at the end of this section. To help with planning an assembly, other ideas and suggested stories are included here. These songs have been chosen because they 'go well' in assembly as the children pick them up readily and enjoy singing them. The songs convey a good clear message and the words and music are of a suitable quality.

Fit for life (*Fit for Life*, 5)
Keeping fit.
A Piece of Cake, Jill Murphy (Walker, 1989).

I've got a body (*Tinderbox*, 5)
Active song, links with senses/health week.
'Mr Wolf and his tail' by Leila Berg, in *Folk Tales* (Brockhampton, 1966).

I like vegetables (*Fit for Life*, 12)
Healthy eating.
A lively, fun song.
Oliver's Vegetables, Vivian French (Hodder, 1995).

So great (*Fit for Life*, 10)
God knows (Luke 12:6-7).
Retell Bible story, e.g. 'Sparrows don't cost much', page 24 in *Listen*, A. J. McCallan (HarperCollins, 1997).

He'll be there (*Songs for Every Assembly*, 44)
Catchy reggae style.
God always near (Psalm 139).
Story of Jesus calming the storm (Mark 4:35-41).

Over the Earth (*Someone's Singing*, 10)
God over all.
Make a picture chart to sing from.
Retell creation story.

Now Jesus one day (*Someone's Singing*, 30)
Alternate singing the song with retelling Bible stories (Mark 4:1 and John 21:1-12).

It happens each spring (*Harlequin*, 15)
New life – Easter.
Horton's Egg, Dr Zeuss (HarperCollins, 1998) or *Titch* (when he plants a sunflower seed), Pat Hutchings (Red Fox, 1997).
See also 'Spring and new life' (page 64), a puppet story.

Look for signs (*Someone's Singing*, 54)
Use display of bright autumn flowers and/or an OHPT.
Read a poem, e.g. 'Little brown seed' (page 14, *Round and Round the Seasons*) – Pat Wynne Jones (Lion, Oxford, 1999).

Paint box (*Harlequin*, 32)
Autumn colours and vegetables.
Make a collection of seeds and fruit.

Milk bottle tops (*Someone's Singing*, 17)
Care for our world.
Hold a litter hunt.
Noah and the Space Ark, Laura Cecil (Hamish Hamilton, 1998).

Who built the ark? (*Someone's Singing*, 54)
Retell story of Noah, Part 1 (Genesis 6 and 7).

I wonder (*Every Colour*, 12)
Questions on natural world.
Read a poem, e.g. 'I wonder', Jeannie Kirby (page 57, *Oxford Treasury of Children's Poems*).

Sing a rainbow (*Apusskidu*, 5)
An old favourite.
Retell story of Noah, Part 2 (Genesis 8 and 9).

Count to ten (*Fit for Life*, 2)
Self-control.
Angry Arthur, Hiawyn Oram (Red Fox, 1993).
Useful illustrations.

Magic penny (*Allelujah!*, 10)
Giving love.
Retell story of Good Samaritan (Luke 10:35-47) or read a recent news item about someone who showed compassion.

A house is a house (*Tinder Box*, 13)
Read a poem, e.g. 'Animals' houses' by James Reeves (page 87, *Oxford Treasury of Children's Poems*).

Living and learning (*Songs for Every Assembly*, 15)
Natural cycles.
An African feel.
Look for things that are changing.

Together (*Songs for Every Assembly*, 7)
Benefit and fun of doing things together.
Mouse and Elephant, An Vrombaut (Hodder Children's, 2000).

How many people (*Tinder Box*, 19)
Family life.
'Baby' by Paul Rogers, a delightful poem (page 52, *Another Very First Poetry Book*, ed. John Forster, Oxford University Press, 1992).

Works calypso (*Tinder Box*, 23)
Keeping busy.
Farmer Duck, Martin Wadell (Walker, 1990) or *Follow the Ants* (based on Proverbs 6:6-11), page 29 in Brian Ogden's book of the same name (Bible Reading Fellowship, 1999).

Slowly walks my grandad (*Tinder Box*, 28)
This song fits well with excerpts from *The Patchwork Quilt*, Valerie Flournoy and Jerry Pinkney (Puffin Picture, 1985).
Learning from elderly/family help.

Thank you for my friends (*Tinder Box*, 31)
The Lonely Prince, Max Bollinger (Methuen, 1981) and/or 'I'm really sorry, said Sarah' from page 29, *It's a Big Family*, Brian Ogden (Bible Reading Fellowship, 1999). And/or *Norma no friends*, Paula Metcalfe (Barefoot Books, 1999).
A theme for a week?

We can do anything (*Game Songs with Professor Dogg's Troupe*, 36)
Encouragement.
Retell story of the 'Ugly Duckling', or read 'The story of the troublesome trucks' from *James the Red Engine* by Rev. W. Awdry (Heinemann, 1998).

Stick on a smile (*Every Colour*, 43)
Can be trite. So point out that some children are unable to smile, which helps so much in life. Tell them in your own words about Bill Magee '. . . a plastic surgeon, who was shocked to find that in Third World countries many children go through life with cleft palates that never get treated. They

cannot smile, and their lips curl open in a constant sneer, making them the object of ridicule. Magee and his wife organised a programme called Operation Smile – plane-loads of doctors and support personnel travel to places like Vietnam, the Philippines, Kenya, Russia and the Middle East, in order to repair facial deformities. So far, they have operated on more than 36,000 children, leaving behind a legacy of children's smiles!' A wonderful story recounted in *What's So Amazing About Grace?*, Phillip Yancey (Zondervan, 1997).

More songs to consider

Don't be a woolly head, *Fit for Life*, 3

I love the sun, *Someone's Singing*, 12

Sing Hosanna, *Allelujah!*, 3

This little light, *Allelujah!*, 14 (you will probably need to explain, it's about people)

When I grow up, *Fit for Life*, 15

If you're happy, *Apusskidu*, 1 (one for the youngest)

He's got the whole world, *Every Colour*, 19

Friends, *Sing a Silver Lining*, 15

Look in the mirror, page 18, *Rock the Baby* by Sheila Wilson (Redhead Music, Marlow, Bucks). Celebrating difference.

Music books referred to

Allelujah!, A. & C. Black, London, 1988

Apusskidu, A. & C. Black, London, 1975

Every Colour, Ward Lock, London, 1983

*Fit for Life by Paul Field, ICC, Eastbourne, 1995

Harlequin, A. & C. Black, London, 1981

Game Songs with Professor Dogg's Troupe, A. & C. Black, London, 1983

*Sing a Silver Lining, A. & C. Black, Huntingdon, 1998

*Songs for Every Assembly, Out of the Ark, Esher, 1998

Someone's Singing, Lord, A. & C. Black, London, 1974

Tinder Box, A. & C. Black, London, 1982

Kidsource and *Kidsource 2* (Kevin Mayhew Ltd) contain hundreds of children's songs and a thematic index which will be helpful when choosing songs upon which to base an assembly.

* Recordings of songs and backing tracks available on CD or tape.

Using narratives

Stories invite participation and can be healing, comforting, affirming, illuminating or challenging, affecting children differently.

A good narrative, whether prose or verse, can be enjoyed for its own sake. It will also speak for itself, so introduction and comment should be kept to a minimum.

Jesus was an excellent storyteller and often concluded with a brief punchline or question. He also waited for questions to come from his listeners.

It is probably more appropriate to consider the follow-up of assembly stories as an activity for the classroom, where more time is available for each child with adults they know well. Children retelling a story together, in their own words, is a useful and interesting experience, revealing their own priorities and concerns. This helps in choosing further narratives to be shared together. Some of the books may also be useful in literacy time.

We have given brief comments on the books recommended here, to help you find what interests you and your children. Most of the narratives have been used in infant-only assemblies. They appear in alphabetical order of author.

When sharing a story in assembly, vary what you do so that the children's attention is maintained. Try not to be predictable! The approach should enhance the narrative, which really is using you as a means of communication.

Some suggestions

- For a story like the Good Samaritan, move from one side of the hall to the other and enact the story. Use different parts of the hall.

- Retell the story in your own way. This best suits folk tales and traditional stories that allow some variation. You will need to practise, though.

- Work together with other teachers to tell a story that involves several characters talking to each other.

- Read the story over three or four consecutive assemblies if arrangements in your school allow. This applies to any length tale, as long as there are suitable points at which to stop each time. There is a selection of longer books listed on page 58.

- Give parts to children to speak from memory, especially repetitive lines or a child character.

- Reading in assembly for children is often difficult, but the more expressive readers can be involved in reading a part of a narrative when suitable. Children can also appear more easily from small hidden places on cue!

- Tell the story to a backing track of selected music or sounds.

- Look at the scripted assemblies in this book to see if there is an approach you can copy or adapt in telling the story of your choice.

- Pose a brief question *before reading the story* in order to help the children focus on a particular person or point, e.g. 'Why do the people in our story today have to work so hard?'

- End with a question for the children to think about as they leave, e.g. 'Which of these men was the really good builder?' (Mark 7:24-29)

- Ask all the children together to mime a part of the story with you, e.g. planting a seed/swaying in the breeze/ marching as soldiers.

- Recount a real-life experience about yourself, a member of the family or a pet.

When reading or telling a story

- Change your voice patterns/speeds.

- Use character differences (mannerisms, ways of speaking).

- Communicate with face and body, or just hands.

- If reading, still make eye contact often.

- Engage your emotions in order to reach the children's.

- For mysterious, enchanting, thoughtful stories, sit well back in your seat, drawing the children into the story with you.

- Emphasise contrasts, e.g. a loud strong voice for the storm, followed by a whisper for the calm.

- Give all you can on the day to your delivery.

Suggested stories

BAUMGART, Klaus, *Laura's Star* (Magi, 1998). Sharing your secrets.

BECK, Ian, *The Ugly Duckling* (Orchard Picture Books, 1987). A nicely illustrated retelling.

BOLLINGER, Max, *The Lonely Prince* (Methuen, 1981).

BROWN, Anthony, *The Tunnel* (Walker, 1997). For older infants – use pictures – girl helps brother.

BROWN, Eileen, *No Problem* (Walker, 1999). Great detailed illustrations. Amusing. Animals try their hand at a construction kit and one finds the instructions.

BUTTERWORTH, Nick, & INKPEN, Mike, *Stories Jesus Told* (Marshall Pickering, 1994).

CECIL, Laura, *Noah and the Space Ark* (Hamish Hamilton, 1998). Pollution/care for wildlife/rescue. Links with song 'Milk Bottle Tops' (see page 50).

DANN, Penny, *The Wheels on the Bus* (Little Orchard, 1998). One for the early years.

DOHERTY, Bertie, *Paddiwak and Cosy* (Little Mammoth, 1988).

DUNBAR, Joyce, & BLYTHE, Gary, *This Is the Star* (Picture Corgi, 1998). Nativity story 'a visual treat'. Text builds up and children could join in.

FRENCH, Vivian, *Oliver's Vegetables* (Hodder, 1995).

FOREMAN, Michael, *Dinosaurs and All That Rubbish* (Picture Puffin, 1974).

GRETZ, Susannah, *The Bears Who Stayed Indoors* (Puffin, 1972).

HUGHES, Shirley, *Giving* (Walker, 1995). A helpful book, including feeling like giving a smack or not! Others in the series.

HUGHES, Shirley, *Alfie Gives a Hand* (Collins Picture Lions, 1983). One of a favourite series.

HUGHES, Shirley, *Dogger* (Red Fox, 1983). Lost friend returns due to unselfish sister. Also on video.

HUTCHINGS, Pat, *Titch* (Red Fox, 1997). See page 50 for a suggested song linking with theme of 'new life'.

INKPEN, Mick, *The Blue Balloon* (Hodder, 1989). A tale of wonder with a magical end.

KERR, Judith, *Mog and Bunny* (Collins Picture Lions, 1991). One of a popular series. A story of faithfulness.

MATTHEWS, Caitlin, *The Blessing Seed* (Barefoot Books, 1998). For older infants, a creation myth with exuberant patterns. Some words may need explaining – for two assemblies?

McKEE, David, *Not Now, Bernard* (Oliver & Boyd, 1991). Listening to one another. Available in BIG book.

MEDEARIS, Angela Shelf, *Too Much Talk* (Walker, 1995). Based on Ghanaian folk tale.

METCALFE, Paula, *Norma No Friends* (Barefoot Books, 1999). Struggling to find a friend. Bold collage pictures. A longer read. Links with song 'Thank you for my friends' (see page 51).

MONKS, Lydia, *I Wish I Were a Dog* (Mammoth, 1998). Different gifts and being me.

MURPHY, Jill, *The Last Noo-Noo* (Walker, 1995). Exhilaratingly funny pictures.

MURPHY, Jill, *A Piece of Cake* (Walker, 1989).

ORAM, Hiawyn, *Angry Arthur* (Red Fox, 1993). Links with song 'Count to ten' (see page 50). Why shatter your world?

SHELDON, Dyane, & BLYTHE, Gary, *The Whale's Song* (Red Fox, 1993). Unusual illustrations. Call of the wild.

SIMMONS, Jane, *Come on, Daisy* (Walker, 1998). Feeling secure and safe.

SIMON, Francesca, & MELLING, David, *What's That Noise?* (Hodder, 1996). Harry is sleeping over and hears strange sound. Reassuring.

SWEETLAND, Nancy, & STEVENS, Rick, *God's Quiet Things* (Lion, 1997). Gentle rhyming text and soft pastel illustrations.

THURY, Frederick H., *The Last Straw* (Zero to Ten Ltd, 1999). Proud camel chosen to carry gifts to Jesus. Brilliantly detailed watercolour pictures. A longer story, well worth reading on its own.

VROMBAUT, An, *Mouse and Elephant* (Hodder Children's, 2000). Finding a way to play together – wonderful. Links with song 'Together' (see page 51).

WADDELL, Martin, *Farmer Duck* (Walker, 1995). Who does the work? Available in BIG book.

WADDELL, Martin, *Once There Were Giants* (Walker, 1989). Growing up.

WADDELL, Martin, *The Owl Babies* (Walker, 1992). Available in BIG book. Care and security in a family, even when we're worried. Connects with children's feelings.

WADDELL, Martin, *We Love Them* (Walker, 1990). Deals carefully with death in the family.

WADDELL, Martin, *When the Teddy Bears Came* (Walker, 1994). Looking after baby together.

WISHINSKY, Frieda, & THOMPSON, Carol, *Oonga, Boonga, Big Brother's Magic Words* (Picture Corgi, 1999). Ask one another – why do these words work?!

Collections of stories

AMNESTY INTERNATIONAL, *Dare to be Different* (Bloomsbury Publishing, 1999), especially page 16, 'Butterflies and swimmers' by Susan Gates and Peter Sutton.

BERG, Leila, *Folk Tales* (Brockhampton, 1966).

DUDLEY-SMITH, Timothy, *Stories of Jesus* (Lion, 1986). Still the best retelling of Bible stories to read out loud to *older* infants.

HEATHFIELD, Rachel, *Beginning with God* (Bible Reading Fellowship, 2000). One of series for 5-7 year olds.

HUGHES, Ted, *How the Whale Became and Other Stories* (Young Puffin, 1963 and many reprints). Interesting for *older* infants to talk about. Longer stories.

McCALLAN, A. J., *Listen! Themes from the Bible Retold for Children* (HarperCollins, 1997).

MOONEY, Bel, *I Wish* (1995), *It's Not Fair* (1989), *It's Not My Fault* (1999) (Mammoth). Series of stories about Kitty, several in each book. Thought provoking and pithy.

OGDEN, Brian, *Follow the Ants* (1999), *Too Busy to Listen* (1998), *It's a Big Family* (Lord's Prayer) (1999) (Barnabas, Bible Reading Fellowship). There are others in this 'Story Mat' series also, designed for *younger* infants, and each includes responsive prayers with Bible stories retold in a school context.

PEARCE, Philippa, *Here Comes Tod* (Walker, 1999). Six stories about a 6 year old. 'Tod and the visitor' (friendship) and 'Tod and the birthday present' (someone special) in particular. Longer stories.

WEBB, Kaye (compiler), *Let the Sun Shine,* a read-aloud collection (Frances Lincoln, 1998). Includes 'The sandboat' by Bertie Doherty – an imaginative journey (page 22); 'Secrets' by Betsy Byars – learning to keep them (page 30); 'When you are six' by Sheila Lavelle (page 62). These are longer stories, but the book contains short pieces and poems.

Longer stories

These are probably best read over three to four days.

COWELL, Cressida, *Don't Do That, Kitty Kilroy* (Hodder, 1999). A cautionary tale; colourful pictures.

FLOURNOY, Valerie, & PINKNEY, Jerry, *The Patchwork Quilt* (Picture Puffin, 1985). Living in a family. Thoughtful. Links with song 'Slowly walks my grandad' (see page 51).

HARTMAN, Bob, *Cheer Up, Chicken* (Lion, 1998). Effective approach to giving and receiving.

MARTIN, Francesca, *The Honey Hunters* (Wayland, 1992). Traditional tale from Africa about sharing. The ending will probably be the talking point.

PARK, Julie, *John Porter in Big Trouble* (Lion, 1990). Feeling guilty/saying sorry/forgiveness and love.

VANN, Donna Reid, *Roberto and the Magical Fountain* (Lion, 1988) and *Stefan's Secret Fear* (Lion, 1990).

Other useful books

AMOS, Janine, 'Feelings' series (Cherry Tree Books, 1993). Helpful material, e.g. afraid, angry, brave, hurt, jealous, sad.

HUGHES, Shirley, *Out and About Through the Year* (Walker, 1988). E.g. misty/hoping/why isn't it dark at bedtime?/the seasons/sick.

WATER, Mark, *A Prayer a Day* (Paternoster, 1998).

Children Just Like Me (Dorling Kindersley, 1995). A book of information and pictures from around the world.

Suggested poems

(Also see page 68)

'Little brown seed' by Rodney Bennett, page 14, *Round and Round the Seasons*, compiled by Pat Wynne Jones (Lion, 1997).

'I like the world' by Steve Turner, page 11, link with 'materials' and us; 'The wind' by Kirsty Topping (aged 7), page 25. Both in *Poems and Prayers for a Better World*, ed. Su Box and Felicity Henderson (Lion, 1999).

'Half-way down' by A. A. Milne (a special safe place) in *When We Were Very Young*, page 81 (Methuen, 1965).

'First and last' by June Crebbin, page 25 in her book, *The Puffin Book of Fantastic First Poems* (Puffin, 1999). About life in the playground.

'My goldfish' by Marie Brookes, page 10, *Yellow Poetry Paintbox*, ed. John Forster (Oxford University Press, 1994). The perfect pet?

'Baby' by Paul Rogers, page 52 (on the way, but who?); 'Coming home' by Eric Finney, page 64 (written as Mum, but could be anyone); 'Surprises' by Jean Conder Soule, page 90 (pressies or?). Three lovely poems to start assembly topics, from *Another Very First Poetry Book*, ed. John Forster (Oxford University Press, 1992).

As well as the poetry books listed above, the following may well also be of assistance:

The Oxford Treasury of Children's Poems, compiled by Michael Harrison and Christopher Stuart-Clarke (1988).

Fizzy Wizzy Poetry Book, John Cuncliffe (Scholastic Young Hippo, 1995).

Red Poetry Paintbox, ed. John Forster (Oxford University Press, 1994).

First Poems, compiled by Julia Eccleshare (Orchard, 1993).

Out of the Blue, Hiawyn Oran (Picture Lion, 1992).

The Puffin Book of Utterly Brilliant Poetry, ed. Brian Patten (1998).

Some suggested Bible stories

Retelling the stories in your own way to suit your audience is the best method. But this means reading and rereading the text to ensure both accuracy and confidence.

The Good News Bible and The Contemporary English Version are recommended. We suggest that when reading directly from the Bible, you select short passages. The Lion Story Bible (50 separate titles in all) is a valuable resource, as is The Children's Bible (Lion, Oxford, 1992). The series by Nick Butterworth and Mick Inkpen, *Stories Jesus Told* (Marshall-Pickering, 1994), is also very good.

Old Testament ideas

Creation (Genesis 1 and 2); Noah and the ark (Genesis 6-9); Moses (Exodus 2-5 and 13-14); Samuel and Eli (1 Samuel 1-3); David and Goliath (1 Samuel 17); Ruth and Naomi (Ruth).

New Testament ideas

The birth of Jesus (Matthew 1 and Luke 2); Zacchaeus (Luke 19:1-9); Parable of the lost sheep (Luke 15); Feeding the 5000 (John 6:1-15); Story of the Good Samaritan (Luke 10:25-37); Jesus calms the storm (Mark 4:35-41); Jesus heals Jairus' daughter (Luke 8:40-56).

Presentation strategies

A hall with lots of other children and grown-ups plus the need to sit quietly and to listen is all quite a challenge for children and teachers. Try to make assembly an encouraging experience for all, and make it easier for the children to listen than to seek alternative amusement.

Clear and engaging language
Words can:
- Paint pictures, 'On the grass there are little drops of water sparkling in the sun.'
- Evoke feelings, 'Only three weeks until Christmas.'
- Provoke interest, 'You'll never guess what . . .'
- Warn, 'I hardly like to tell you, but . . .'
- Include, 'I want you all to help me keep a nice secret.'

Depending on the response needed we can speak quietly, mysteriously, smilingly, disappointedly, etc., to keep the children with us, sharing our feelings.

Something interesting to look at
Each child needs to see well enough to avoid disappointment and unrest so anything that is big, clear and in keeping with the topic, will be fine, e.g. large pictures/a tank of fish or tadpoles.

Sounds and other senses
As well as recorded music and sound, live music, even the simplest kind, is very interesting. Many children will be planning to 'have a go' even as they watch and listen.

Using a candle that smells nice is calming. Children are happy to watch and share this experience, taking it in and also remembering similar experiences.

Watching someone eat an apple is interesting because it is familiar. Watching someone eat wheat grains is interesting because it is possibly a new idea.

Describing sensations also evokes memories, e.g. stroking a cat's silky coat or picking blackberries.

Watching others present a drama or action
Even a short simple one is interesting because there is movement. A short story narrated by the teacher and acted out by some children is usually most acceptable. 'Dressing up' is always very exciting.

Varying the children's seating arrangements

This allows for different types of presentations; a large circle offering the children a good view of the middle as there may be only 2-3 rows, and in lines for something like a picture or puppet play. The teacher can change the point of focus by moving about, side to side, standing up or sitting down.

Finger plays

Simple drama using hands and mimed responses can engage everyone. Just for a minute or two, a sequence of mime or finger actions carried out in silence can regain wandering attention! E.g. 'Incy Wincy Spider' or 'There's the church, here's the steeple'. Miming, e.g. stroking a cat/sewing a patch/opening a parcel/ hitting a ball/ pretending to watch something land on your hand.

Visitors

People with something new to show and tell are usually very well received. Each school will have its own local speakers who would be pleased to come – police, coastguards, road safety officer, artist, librarian, nurse, etc. Children of different nationality could invite their parents to come and share some of their culture and tradition.

Repetition

When so much is being presented that is new and possibly challenging, to hear familiar words and take part in familiar actions is very satisfying. To give examples would be difficult, as each school has its own little traditions. Maybe a special hand-signal for getting everyone's attention, a birthday song, or something invented for a particular purpose, like a rhyme or spoken response.

Entertainment

There is an element of entertainment in all presentations, but, yes, just occasionally, go for it. Make it enjoyable, funny, even serious but thought provoking, and it will be remembered for quite a while. The children will know that assembly can be 'really great' – not every day, but who knows, maybe again soon. For example, re-enacting a pantomime story like *Cinderella*.

To restore attention

This game could be used. Three claps then teacher does an action. Children must quickly copy, e.g. clap, clap, clap, touch head, clap, clap, clap, wiggle fingers, etc.

Use familiar classroom equipment

Use familiar equipment (perhaps for a new purpose) to illustrate a story or teaching, e.g. large construction kit or something from the house corner.

Link items without pausing

You could even link items without a pause or comment, running straight into the next one. At the end of a story or song, children often feel the need to comment or move about. If they can join together in an action or other response you will all be 'moving in the same direction'.

Dialogue

Dialogue is interesting. Two points of view could be aired; hold a short discussion, make a prepared plan or even try to solve a small, but immediate problem. This is modelling considerate conversation, with perhaps questions and answers. Speakers could be adult/adults, child/adult, etc. Some of these ideas are helpful to new teachers, as their introduction to taking part in assembly.

Vary the elements of an assembly

This is as important as in the classroom. Contrast listening to a poem with an activity; follow intensive singing of a song with something to sit and watch.

Using a puppet

Building up the character over a long period, e.g. once a term for two years.

Children find puppets very interesting and their power to hold everyone's attention is awesome. It can be quite disconcerting for a teacher to be upstaged by their own puppet – this can happen, so be prepared!

The first choice to be made is what messages do you want to convey? Probably the two main types would be acting out a narrative or encouraging good behaviour and attitudes. The puppets could be of any type and there could be a whole cast of them, or just one. They may have their own voices or may whisper to the puppeteer, who passes on the message. It may be a one-off performance or a character that pops up from time to time. It's your own choice.

There is no escaping the fact that careful thinking and preparation are essential. Every word and action needs to be rehearsed, together with the management of simple props. It has to be semi-automatic because in front of a very live audience there is little room for error. The children will laugh at any mistake. But when the story or dialogue is going as planned, the children will be intensely involved, associating, feeling, responding if asked, empathising whole-heartedly. The youngest ones will almost believe the puppet is real. The fact that they can see the puppeteer working it counts for nothing. The memory of the story or conversation will stay with them long after they have left the hall and the content can be used and built upon later in class as teachers wish. An example:

Spring and new life – Glove puppet bear 'S' who speaks only to 'P' the puppeteer, is the young friend of the puppeteer.

Scene begins with P approaching S's house (a table), knocks on door and sits down (put puppet on hand). S appears from below the table and talks to P, then returns below.

P explains to audience that S is gardening and won't be long. (Banging, scraping from below the table.) S comes up carrying a pot with a dead-looking plant. Puts it on table and begins to cry.

Conversation between P and S. P reports what S says to the children. S thinks the plant is not alive and P reassures S that the plant is not dead, but will grow again soon, now it is spring.

S is not convinced so P says he/she knows a wonderful story in the Bible all about coming back to life. S settles down to listen and then notices the children. S looks slowly around the audience and then asks P if they like stories too. P reports back and says, 'Oh yes'.

A version of Jesus' death and resurrection written for children (or retold by teacher) can be read. S and P finish with a conversation that reflects the joy and wonder of the story and the hope that the plant will sprout again. (When it does, perhaps in a few weeks, it can be shown in assembly with or without the puppet.) S can wave goodbye to P and also children if appropriate and is put back under the table.

In this piece there were two parallel threads on a common theme: S's experience and learning and the Bible account of Jesus' death and resurrection. This format can be used with different content, e.g. 'the two sons who helped/did not help their father' (it's what you do that counts); 'The house on the rock' (building a house and building your life); the Good Samaritan (actively helping each other).

For large, handmade puppets:

Children Worldwide, 'Dalesdown', Honeybridge Lane, Dial Post, Horsham, West Sussex, RH13 8NX.
Tel. 01403 710712

Ways in which children can participate

The overall aims are to be inclusive, to keep the pace moving as the teacher wishes to keep to the point (without unwanted digressions) and for the assembly to be enjoyed by all.

- Ask a question, and ask for a show of hands to answer. Explain that when the answer is given everyone who thinks the same should smile and nod. One child is asked to give an answer.

- Ask a question and ask for a show of hands to answer. Everyone with hands up speaks out together (this would have to be an easy, obvious question).

- Begin an explanation or story, pausing for children to supply the next word all together.

- Have a yes/no show of hands (this for giving opinions or answering closed questions).

- For a numerical answer, ask the children to raise the correct number of fingers.

- Repeat phrases or important words after the teacher. New information, expressions or words can be taught in assembly and need rehearsing right away if they are to be learnt, e.g. Jerusalem or cocoon; descriptive words.

- Repeat actions, following teacher in silence. This can be a known finger-play rhyme or a message the teacher wants to convey, e.g. finger to lips, point to music centre, cup hands round ears or count down fingers from 10 to zero (in silence) before starting the next item.

- Respond to a previously agreed hand-signal.

- A recognised system of hand-signing could be used (e.g. Makaton) to validate alternative methods of communication.

- Before a song, the teacher could start a pattern of claps, the children join in and at a given signal, go straight into a song.

- Use silence as a positive activity. Explain to the children that silence is achieved when nothing is moving (this is good science). Make it clear that they must keep every part of their body still (even their eyes) and then they will hear the silence. (Sometimes sounds from outside will be heard, this may or may not be useful.) Being able to keep silent is especially good before and after a song and is excellent training for the performance of any music. Children enjoy 'making the silence' together in this way.

- Brainstorming – a variety of one-word answers from as many children as possible, if the topic in hand demands this. Not to be used too often in assembly.

- Before asking a question, name the child or children to answer it, e.g. 'Let's see if . . . can tell us . . .' (knowing she/he certainly can).

Whatever strategy is being used, smiles and encouragement are always important and all children's legitimate responses should be clearly valued and appreciated.

More ideas and suggestions

- Ask a family of the school or a local leader of another religious group to be involved in holding an assembly of worship in a different tradition. If you are in a multi-ethnic area and wish to do this, we feel this is the best way. Compulsory teaching of other religions is part of the National Curriculum and should not be confused with assembly.

- Gradually undo and line-up a set of babushka dolls (or similar) and move into the theme of size/things within things/inside and outside. Link with either 'The flower of happiness' (page 84, John Cuncliffe's *Fizzy Wizzy Poetry Book*) or a traditional song like 'This is the house that Jack built', or 'All in a wood there was a tree', or 'There was an old woman who swallowed a fly'.

- Contact Christian Aid for some very useful resources, e.g. *Shampa Lives in India* – a colourful lovely BIG book about life and customs; 'Give it Away', stories of real-life children around the world, showing the gifts we share (free leaflet). Both come with activity suggestions.
  Contact Christian Aid Resources, PO Box 100, London SE1 7RT, or
  www.christian-aid.org.uk

- Use an OHPT picture as a starting point for an assembly. Sometimes catch the children's attention by showing the picture as they are coming into assembly. You can simply ask them to look carefully first and then go on to ask questions about both what they can see and what they think.

  By using transparencies which are already available from organisations like Tearfund, Oxfam, Christian Aid and Feba, new knowledge from a wider world can be introduced to the children. This is an important facet of assembly.

- Topics taken from children's television programmes or pictures in newspapers can be effectively developed into a meaningful assembly . . . especially if there is a good song to link with it!

- Reading part of a poem several times to allow children just to stop, listen, think and imagine can be very emotive. For example, look at John Cuncliffe's 'Thought of getting into bed', page 13, *Fizzy Wizzy Poetry Book*; or Stanley Cook's 'Crayoning', page 14, *A Very First Poetry Book* (Oxford, 1990).

  The wonderful thing is that the children may well join in with you quite spontaneously.

- Compile ideas in classes on a set pattern to bring and share in assembly, e.g.

  Being safe is . . .

  When we play we must . . .

  I wish I could . . .

  This may well link with your circle time.

- 'Imprints' – signs of where things once were, e.g. leaves in stones → stones on sand → feet on sand → shapes in plasticine → hands on towels – and so on.

  Explain how this idea is used in art and show some examples. It also illustrates how one thing affects another. How do we make impressions in life? By our smiles, our helpfulness, etc.

- Role models – look out for simple modern real-life stories of compassion and care that give positive, valuable examples of achievement, e.g. the story of Bill Magee (quoted on pages 51 and 52) and those young people who go with VSO or other agencies to help with projects like homes for street children in Brazil. There are many stories about people helping others. You may actually know someone personally. If not, watch out for reports in the newspaper or magazines.

Theme index

See pages 55-59 for more details of the books listed.